Keeping Unusual Pets

CHINCHILLAS

Tom Handford

www.heinemann.co.uk/library
Visit our website to find out more information about Heinemann Library books.

To order:
☎ Phone 44 (0) 1865 888066
▤ Send a fax to 44 (0) 1865 314091
▯ Visit the Heinemann Bookshop at www.heinemann.co.uk/library to browse our catalogue and order online.

First published in Great Britain by Heinemann Library, Halley Court, Jordan Hill, Oxford OX2 8EJ
a division of Reed Educational and Professional Publishing Ltd. Heinemann is a registered trademark
of Reed Educational and Professional Publishing Ltd.

OXFORD MELBOURNE AUCKLAND JOHANNESBURG BLANTYRE
GABORONE IBADAN PORTSMOUTH (NH) USA CHICAGO

© Reed Educational and Professional Publishing Ltd 2002
First published in paperback 2003
The moral right of the proprietor has been asserted.

Designed by Celia Floyd
Originated by Dot Gradations Limited
Printed by Wing King Tong in Hong Kong/China

ISBN 0 431 12408 6 (hardback)　　　　ISBN 0 431 12412 4 (paperback)
06 05 04 03 02　　　　　　　　　　　07 06 05 04 03
10 9 8 7 6 5 4 3 2 1　　　　　　　　 10 9 8 7 6 5 4 3 2 1

British Library Cataloguing in Publication Data

Handford, Tom
　Chinchillas. – (Keeping unusual pets)
1. Chinchillas as pets – Juvenile literature
I. Title
636.9'3593

Acknowledgements
The Publishers would like to thank the following for permission to reproduce photographs:
Corbis: p. 4; NHPA: p. 10; Tom Handford: pp. 8 (top), 8 (bottom), 44 (top); Tudor Photography: pp. 5, 6, 7
(top), 7 (bottom), 9 (top), 9 (bottom), 11 (top), 11 (bottom), 12, 13, 14, 15, 16, 17, 18 (top), 18 (bottom), 19,
20, 21 (top), 21 (bottom), 22 (top), 22 (bottom), 23, 24, 25, 26 (top), 26 (bottom), 27 (top), 27 (bottom), 28, 29
(top), 29 (bottom), 30 (top), 30 (bottom), 31, 32, 33 (top), 33 (bottom), 34, 35 (top), 35 (bottom), 36 (top), 36
(bottom), 37, 38, 39, 40, 41, 42, 43, 44 (bottom left), 44 (bottom right), 45.

Cover photograph reproduced with permission of the RSPCA Photo Library/Angela Hampton.

Every effort has been made to contact copyright holders of any material reproduced in this book.
Any omissions will be rectified in subsequent printings if notice is given to the Publishers.

Disclaimer

No animals were harmed during the process of taking photographs for this series.

Contents

Any words appearing in the text in bold, **like this**, are explained in the Glossary.

What is a chinchilla?

Chinchillas are small, plump animals with very soft and beautiful fur. They are **mammals**, which means they are **warm-blooded** (they produce their own body heat), give birth to live babies and feed their babies with milk. Chinchillas are members of the **rodent** family, which includes rats and mice. Rodents have very sharp front teeth for gnawing at their food.

Wild chinchillas

- Wild chinchillas live in South America.
- They live in rocks and **crevices** in the Andes Mountains where it is very cold.
- They have very thick, dense fur to keep them warm.
- They find bark, branches and trees to eat.
- They are inquisitive and want to explore everything they can.
- They love the company of other chinchillas and live together in large family groups.

Chinchillas have very long whiskers, a curly, bushy tail and powerful back legs for hopping and jumping. They use their short front paws to hold their food.

Chinchillas in danger

For centuries, people hunted chinchillas because they wanted to use their fur to make cloaks, hats and trimmings for fine clothes. This meant that chinchillas in South America became **endangered**, and almost died out. Chinchillas are now a **protected species**, and it is forbidden to hunt them. But some chinchillas are still kept on fur farms and **bred** for their fur.

Pet chinchillas

In 1923, a mining engineer working in the Andes Mountains in South America was allowed to take twelve chinchillas home to the USA. He used these animals to breed hundreds more. In fact, almost all the chinchillas sold in pet shops today are descended from these first twelve animals!

Need to know

- Children are not allowed to buy pets themselves. In any case you should always have an adult with you when you buy your pet.
- Most countries have laws that say that pets must be treated with respect. It is your responsibility to make sure your chinchilla is healthy and well cared for. Always take your pet to the vet if it is ill or injured.

Like most chinchillas sold around the world today, this chinchilla is descended from just twelve animals that were brought into the USA in 1923.

Chinchilla facts

Pet chinchillas are different from their wild cousins. For one thing, they are usually larger – a fully-grown adult male or female pet chinchilla weighs from 700 to 1100 grams and is about the size of a small rabbit. (Female chinchillas are usually larger than males.) Pet chinchillas also have better quality fur that comes in a variety of colours.

Amazing colours

- Nearly all wild chinchillas are grey.
- There are now over 20 different colours of pet chinchillas.
- Grey pet chinchillas are known as 'standard' chinchillas.
- Experts have special names for pet chinchillas' colours, such as sapphire, black velvet, brown velvet, pink white, violet, and royal blue.

The picture on the right shows a standard (grey) chinchilla and a pink white chinchilla.

Night-time fun

Chinchillas are **nocturnal** animals, which means that most of their activities take place at night. They race around the walls of their cage and play with pieces of wood or other objects in their cage. They spend most of the day asleep, but they are awake at some times during the day.

This picture shows (from left to right) a Wilson white, a standard, a pink white and a self black chinchilla.

Did you know?

- Some chinchillas live for over twenty years, but most live happily for five to ten years.
- Chinchillas make a lot of different sounds, including a long warning cry when they are afraid.

7

Chinchilla babies

Female chinchillas are pregnant for three and half months and can give birth twice a year. Baby chinchillas are called **kits**. The number of kits born at one time can range from one to four. Sometimes a chinchilla mother gives birth to five or six kits, but this is very rare. When they are first born the kits weigh between 25 and 50 grams.

Did you know?

- Kits are born with fur and their eyes open.
- A few hours after they are born they are able to walk, see and hear.
- After one day they can romp around their cage.
- Kits spend a lot of time **suckling** (drinking milk) from their mother.
- A suckling kit can sometimes injure its mother by biting her.

After just one day, this kit is already being nosy and adventurous. It is covered in soft baby fur.

This chinchilla kit is only a few minutes old. When they are born, baby chinchillas are very wet and soon get cold. They creep under their mother, whose body heat helps to dry them.

8

Weaning

When they are about eight weeks old, baby kits stop suckling from their mother and start to eat solid food. This is called **weaning**. After weaning, pet chinchilla kits start eating pellets and hay. At this age they are independent of their mother and can look after themselves.

By the time they are two months old, kits are ready to be weaned. They can eat solid food and survive without their mother.

This one-year-old chinchilla is fully grown and has its adult fur. Between the age of ten and fifteen months, chinchillas are in their **prime**, which means their fur is at its very best.

9

Is a chinchilla for you?

Chinchillas look beautiful and are great fun to play with, but they need caring for every day. Your pet chinchilla will be your friend if you treat it kindly and look after all its needs, but it will nip or bite you if you are rough with it, or treat it cruelly. A female chinchilla will nip you and spray you with her **urine** if you upset her. This is the way that chinchillas protect themselves in the wild. It should not happen if you treat your chinchilla kindly. The more attention you give to your pet, the more pleasure and fun it will give back to you.

Chinchilla good points

- Chinchillas are easy to look after and they usually stay healthy.
- They are tough little creatures that usually live for a long time.
- They are not expensive to feed.
- There are many colours of chinchilla to choose from.
- Chinchillas do not have a smell.
- Fleas and other insects cannot live in a chinchilla's fur because it is so dense.
- Normally, chinchillas will not bite you if they like you and you pick them up properly.

Chinchillas keep their fur very clean by **grooming** themselves.

Chinchilla not-so-good points

- You cannot take a chinchilla for a walk, as you can a dog or even a ferret.
- You cannot let chinchillas loose in the garden, or when other animals are around.
- If you let chinchillas run around a room you will find droppings wherever they go. However, these droppings are very dry and are easy to clear up.
- Chinchillas need larger cages than small **rodents**, such as hamsters or mice.
- Chinchillas love to gnaw things, so if you let them loose inside your house, you will need to watch out for your furniture and other objects!
- Some people have an **allergy** to chinchilla fur.

Yes or no?

Having a chinchilla for a pet means caring for it every day and always treating it with respect. Think this over carefully before you make the decision to become a chinchilla owner.

A chinchilla can make an excellent pet, but you cannot leave it to roam about your house like you might a cat or a dog.

Chinchillas will gnaw at anything! If you let your pet run free in your house, be very careful that it does not chew on precious things or things that might be bad for it.

11

Choosing a chinchilla

You can buy a chinchilla from your local pet shop or from a specialist **breeder**. It is very easy to make contact with chinchilla breeders. Many of them advertise on the Internet and some have their own websites. You can also look on the Internet for your local chinchilla society. The people at your local society will be able to give you useful information on where to buy chinchillas.

Which one?

- Try to buy a young chinchilla, under six months old.
- Buying a chinchilla that is twelve to sixteen weeks old will mean that it will quickly learn to trust you.
- Both male and female chinchillas make good pets, but some people prefer males. (If you upset a male chinchilla he will only nip or bite you and almost never spray you with **urine**.)
- Standard grey chinchillas are cheaper than coloured chinchillas.
- Do not rush into buying a chinchilla. It is better to wait until you find an animal that is perfect for you in every way.

Always ask to hold the chinchilla you would like to buy. If it is relaxed and friendly it should be a good pet for you.

What to look for

There are a few basic things to look out for when you are choosing your chinchilla.

- The chinchilla should be living in clean surroundings.
- It should have bright eyes, with no sign of wetness around them.
- Its fur should be smooth and shiny, with no roughness or bald patches.
- Its teeth should be straight and not **overgrown**.
- It should be interested in you, and not nervous.

Teeth problems

Look very carefully at your chinchilla's teeth to check that they are straight and not overgrown. Ask the pet shop owner or chinchilla breeder to check the chinchilla's teeth for **malocclusion**. Chinchillas suffering from this condition have teeth that grow too long and are bent or **deformed**.

This chinchilla has good teeth that are the right length and nice and straight. Chinchillas' teeth should be slightly yellow like this.

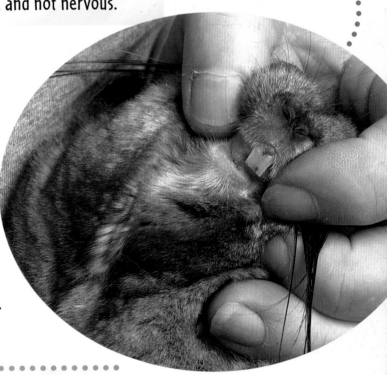

Top tip

Make sure the chinchilla that you choose does not chew its fur. A chinchilla with patches of very short chewed fur will not make a good pet. It will always be very nervous, and never look as beautiful as one with perfect fur.

13

One chinchilla or two?

Should you keep just one chinchilla or a pair? The answer to this question is up to you and your family. Many people have only one chinchilla and both the pet and its owners seem happy with this arrangement. If you have never owned a chinchilla before, it is probably best to start with just one.

If you do decide to keep two chinchillas, here are some things to think about:

- Make sure you have a cage that is big enough for two animals to live in comfortably.
- It is best to buy two males or two females.
- When you are choosing your male or female pair, try to buy brothers or sisters. They will be used to living together and should be happy to share a cage.
- If you keep a male and female together they will probably breed and have young. Looking after baby chinchillas is a big task that should only be undertaken by experienced chinchilla keepers.

Even if chinchillas are brothers or sisters, they may take a while to get used to sharing a cage. Stay with them until you are sure that they are getting along together.

Introducing chinchillas

It is possible for two chinchillas that are not brothers or sisters to live together happily, but they may take a while to settle down. Be very careful when you introduce two animals for the first time, in case they fight. One way to do this successfully is to put the two animals in separate cages side by side, about four centimetres apart. That way they can smell and see each other but cannot fight or get hurt. After seven days, the animals will have got to know each other. Now you can put the two animals into one cage. Always try to introduce them in a cage that neither of them has been in before.

If the pair start to fight, put them back into their own cages straight away. Then try to introduce them again another time. If they keep on fighting, you should talk to a chinchilla breeder about finding a new home for one of them.

Take it slowly

Never hurry or be impatient when introducing chinchillas for the first time. If they do not get along they might fight and even kill each other.

It is best to introduce two animals in the morning, because this is the time when they are sleepy and not very active.

15

Your chinchilla's home

You will need the right cage and equipment to keep your chinchilla happy and healthy. You can buy a cage at a pet shop, or from a supplier of chinchilla equipment. Try looking on the Internet for suppliers of cages and equipment or contact your local chinchilla society (see page 47) for help and advice.

Choosing a cage

Chinchilla cages are available in many shapes and sizes, but all good cages are made from 16-gauge quality galvanized wire mesh. You will need to buy an all-wire cage because chinchillas have very sharp teeth and can chew through other materials. Wooden hutches and cages with plastic parts are not suitable.

Inside the cage

Your cage needs:
- a hay rack
- a water bottle container
- a food bowl
- one or two wooden shelves fixed to the back or the side of the cage for your chinchilla to climb onto. Keep the shelves clean. You may need to replace them if your pet has chewed them a lot.

To keep your chinchilla healthy you must give it a good home.

16

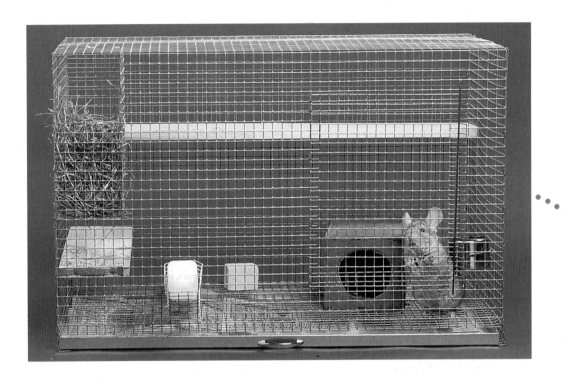

The perfect place

Your chinchilla's cage needs to be placed next to a wall or in the corner of a room. It should also be raised above the ground. The cage should not be positioned in direct sunlight or too close to a radiator because your chinchilla will get too hot.

Top tip

Never put your chinchilla's cage in the middle of a room. Your pet will not know which side of its cage you will appear from next. This will make it feel very nervous.

A cage measuring 50 cm wide × 50 cm deep × 46 cm high would be suitable for keeping one chinchilla. For two chinchillas you will need a cage measuring 92 cm wide × 38 cm deep × 46 cm high, like the one shown above. Chinchillas do not need very tall cages because they are rock hoppers rather than climbers. However, they do enjoy having plenty of space, so even if you have only one pet, buy a bigger cage if you can afford it.

Food containers

Your chinchilla's food container does not need to be very big – it only has to hold a couple of tablespoons of pellets. The most important thing is that your pet should not be able to tip it up! It should either be too heavy for your pet to move or it should be held in place by a **retaining clip** attached to the wall of the cage.

When your chinchilla eats pellets it will pick them up with its teeth but then hold them in one paw while chewing.

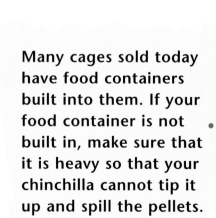

Many cages sold today have food containers built into them. If your food container is not built in, make sure that it is heavy so that your chinchilla cannot tip it up and spill the pellets.

Water bottles

The best water container for your pet is a plastic bottle that hangs on the outside of its cage. You can buy these bottles from pet shops. Water bottles come in a variety of sizes. A medium-sized bottle should fit the retaining clip fitted to your cage.

It is not a good idea to have a water bowl inside your chinchilla's cage because the water can easily get dirty from droppings, waste food or **urine**. Dirty water can make your pet very ill.

Chinchillas love to chew, so some protection around the water bottle is essential. If your cage does not have a wire holder for the bottle, put a small piece of sheet metal between the water bottle and the cage.

Change the water in the bottle every day. If the water from your tap at home is good enough for you to drink then it is good enough for your pet!

Top tip

Sometimes your pet's water bottle will get dirty inside. To clean the bottle:

- Put a little coarse sand into the bottle.
- Half fill the bottle with warm water.
- Place your finger or thumb over the opening and give the bottle a good shake.
- Wash the bottle in the normal way, but if you use soapy water make sure that you rinse it carefully.

Dust baths

Did you know that in the wild chinchillas take regular dust baths? They roll around in dust or sand to get their fur clean. Your chinchilla will need to take a dust bath two or three times a week to keep its fur in good condition.

Buying a bath

Your chinchilla's bath should be made from **galvanized** (rust-proof) metal and should be big enough for your pet to fit inside it comfortably. You can buy metal dust baths from pet shops or from suppliers of chinchilla equipment. Do not give your chinchilla a plastic bath because it may chew or even eat it. Plastic is very bad for chinchillas. They cannot digest it and it can eventually kill them.

Chinchillas like to take a dust bath in the evening. Let your pet bathe for about fifteen minutes, then take the dust bath out of its cage.

Bathing in sand

- Your chinchilla will need a special sort of sand, called sepolita sand. You can buy it from good pet shops.

- Pour about 3 centimetres of sand into the bottom of the bath.

- Leave your chinchilla for about fifteen minutes in its bath. It will love to roll around!

- After your chinchilla has had its bath, or if the sand is soiled, you should sieve it through a very fine mesh sieve.

- The sieved sand can be kept in the bath ready for the next time.

- Sepolita sand can be used again and again, but you should change it every few months.

Chewing fun

Chinchillas love to chew at things, and chewing helps them to wear down their teeth, which are always growing. To provide your pet with plenty of chewing exercise, you can give it small pieces of white, soft wood, such as pine. The pieces should be about 20 centimetres long.

Some pet shops sell special wooden blocks for chinchillas, or you could give your chinchilla a small block of unvarnished pine floorboard, or a piece of a branch cut from a sweet apple tree. Ask an adult to check that the wood has not been painted or sprayed with chemicals.

Always sweep your chinchilla's droppings off chewing blocks so they do not get too dirty.

Safety first

Do not give your chinchilla things to chew that it would not find in the wild, such as cuttlefish shells.

Some chinchillas like to chew blocks made of a light rock called pumice stone. You can buy blocks of pumice stone from pet shops. Pumice is full of air bubbles.

Carrying cages

A small carrying cage is a very useful piece of equipment. You can put your pet in it while you are cleaning out its cage, or if you need to make any repairs to the cage. A carrying cage is also very useful if you need to take your pet to the vet, or if you decide to enter your pet for a chinchilla show.

Sleeping boxes

Many chinchilla keepers do not use sleeping boxes. If you have one you will find it harder to attract your chinchilla's attention during the day, when it is asleep in its box. However, if you

This carrying cage is made of galvanized metal mesh. Carrying cages are sometimes also known as show cages because owners use them to take their pets to shows.

do choose to have a sleeping box, make sure it is made from soft white wood, such as pine. The wood should be untreated and you should never use a plastic or metal box. Do not forget to clean the box out every week, because as well as sleeping in it your pet will chew away at it.

If you buy a sleeping box with a roof, try and get one that has entrances at both ends. This means you will be able to attract your pet's attention whichever way it enters its box.

Natural exercise

Your pet chinchilla does not need an exercise wheel in its cage. Wheels are not good for pets with long tails, because their tails can easily get caught in them. Your chinchilla will use the walls of its cage as a race track and run around them very fast. It will usually exercise in the evening, when all chinchillas are wide awake.

Chinchilla equipment

Here is a checklist of all the equipment that your chinchilla will need:

- metal cage with wooden shelves
- food container
- hay rack (which is usually built into the cage)
- water bottle
- dust bath
- chewing blocks
- carrying cage
- sleeping box (optional).

If possible, buy a sleeping box without a roof. Then you will be able to see your pet better!

Caring for your chinchilla

Looking after a pet is a big responsibility. There are some things you will need to do for your chinchilla every day.

- Feed your chinchilla pellets.
- Feed your pet at regular times, for example before you go to school and when you get back home again.
- Place a handful of hay into your chinchilla's hay rack.
- Put fresh water into its water bottle.
- As well as giving your pet food and water, you should make a fuss of it. Talk to your chinchilla and tell it how special it is.
- Always make sure your pet is healthy and happy.

Food pellets

Give your chinchilla food pellets twice a day, in the morning and the evening. You do not need to give it very many – an eggcup-full is fine, but make sure your pet always has some pellets in its bowl. It will like to keep nibbling on them all through the day.

Pellets made especially for chinchillas contain everything that your pet needs. They provide a balanced diet with all the necessary **vitamins**. Do not feed your chinchilla any other pellets, such as rabbit or guinea pig pellets.

Chinchillas never eat a lot at once and they can waste pellets by scattering them around. If this happens, feed your chinchilla fewer pellets but feed it more often.

Top tip

Did you know that changing your chinchilla's diet from one brand of pellets to another can make it ill? Always try to buy the same brand of pellets if possible.

Keep it simple

The only things a chinchilla needs to stay healthy are pellets, hay and water. Never give your pet snacks such as sunflower seed, nuts or crisps.

Just occasionally, it is alright to give your chinchilla a healthy treat, such as a raisin or a very small piece of sweet apple. But do this very rarely. It is better to give your pet no treats at all than to give it too many.

Holiday care

- If you are away for even a couple of days, it is best to ask a friend or neighbour to visit your chinchilla every day.
- Choose someone who knows and likes your chinchilla and who can be trusted to look after your pet for you.
- Ask them to clean out its cage and give it food, hay and water.
- Make sure you leave instructions about how much food to give, and when to feed your pet.
- Leave your phone number and your vet's phone number in case there is an emergency.

You can give your chinchilla a raisin as a very special treat, but make sure you do not do this too often!

Fresh hay

Your chinchilla will enjoy chewing on fresh hay. The hay will give it the **roughage** it needs and it will also have lots of fun throwing the hay around!

- You can buy fresh meadow hay at a pet shop. Just buy one bag at a time.
- Every day, clear out your chinchilla's old hay and put a handful of fresh hay into its hayrack.
- Make sure that the hay you buy is dry and dust free. It should smell sweet. If it has a musty smell, do not feed it to your pet.

Chewing hay will keep your chinchilla happy for hours.

Cleaning the cage

It is very important to clean your chinchilla's cage, shelves and chewing blocks every week. Cleaning out its cage is not difficult. Simply wipe over the inside and outside of the cage with warm soapy water. Then rinse it with clean water. Do the same for the shelves and chewing blocks if they are dirty.

After you have cleaned everything in the cage, rinse it thoroughly with clean water. Make sure that the cage is completely dry before you put your pet back in.

Removing waste

All chinchilla cages should have a waste tray, which fits directly underneath the cage. This is to catch all your pet's waste and droppings. Place a newspaper in the waste tray. At the end of each day, roll up the old newspaper covered in droppings and waste. Throw it away in a safe place. Replace it with another piece of clean newspaper. If the tray is wet with **urine**, wipe it dry. Always wash your hands after cleaning your chinchilla's cage.

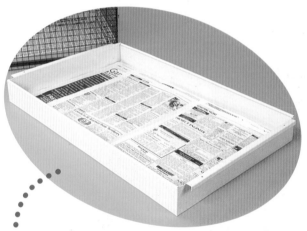

You should replace the newspaper in the bottom of the waste tray every day. Remember to wash your hands after you have done this.

Do not spray!

Never use fly sprays, air fresheners or perfume near your pets. All these sprays are harmful and may poison your chinchilla.

27

Health checks

It is important to check your chinchilla regularly to make sure that it is healthy.

- Are your chinchilla's eyes clear?
- Does its fur look shiny and healthy?
- Does it seem bright and **alert**? Healthy chinchillas are always nosy and want to investigate everything that is going on.

This chinchilla has bright, healthy eyes, with no redness or wet patches around them.

If your pet seems ill ...

If one day you find your chinchilla sitting in the corner of its cage, being very quiet and not taking any interest in what you are doing, then something may be wrong. Make sure that your pet's pellets and water have not been soiled. Check that the droppings in the waste tray are firm and dry. If they are messy and wet, you may have fed your pet some mouldy hay. Do not feed your chinchilla any hay for three to four days, and check your pet regularly to make sure that it is not getting any worse.

Chinchillas are tough little creatures and if they are properly cared for they are hardly ever ill. However, if your chinchilla is ill for more than a day, you should think about taking it to the vet. There is more advice on chinchilla illnesses and how to treat them on pages 36 to 41.

These are normal chinchilla droppings. They are firm and fairly dry, and **cylindrical** in shape.

Keeping cool

Chinchillas have very thick, dense fur. In the winter this keeps them cosy and warm, but in the summer they shed some of their fur. Ideally, the temperature for your pet should not be more than 15°C and should never fall below freezing point. If the temperature reaches as high as 20°C your pet will suffer. You will need to do something fast to lower the temperature. An electric fan will help, and you will find that your chinchilla enjoys the feeling of cool air blowing around it.

If you use an electric fan to cool down your chinchilla, make sure your pet is safely in its cage so that it cannot chew on the electric cable.

Top tip

You will know if your pet is too warm because its ears will become bright pink.

Chinchilla fur

Your pet chinchilla does not need a lot of help to keep its fur in good condition. It will do this itself with dust baths. But there may be times when your chinchilla's fur does not seem to be in very good condition. For example, in the spring, your chinchilla will lose some of its thick winter fur. This is known as **moulting**.

Grooming your pet

If your pet's coat is looking out of condition, you may decide that it needs **grooming**. To groom your chinchilla, you will need a strong metal comb. The type used for long-haired dogs and cats will work well. Some chinchilla owners use a special grooming comb when they are taking their animals to a show, but these combs are too sharp for normal use. Before using one of these special combs you must be taught what to do by an experienced chinchilla keeper.

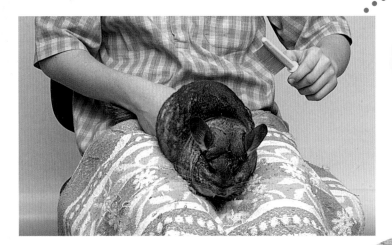

Make sure your chinchilla is happy on your lap before you start to groom it. (For more information on how to handle your chinchilla, see pages 32–33.)

Hold your chinchilla with one hand and use your other hand to comb its fur. Always work from head to tail.

Grooming tips

- Start by sitting on a chair and covering your lap with a towel or cloth.
- Place your pet on your lap, and make a fuss of it to gain its confidence.
- Begin grooming your chinchilla at the neck and head and work down towards the tail.
- Always comb down the body, in the direction that the fur lies.
- Remember to be patient and gentle at all times.

Chinchillas' nails do not need any attention. Your pet will keep its nails short by climbing around in its cage and playing with its pieces of wood and pumice stone.

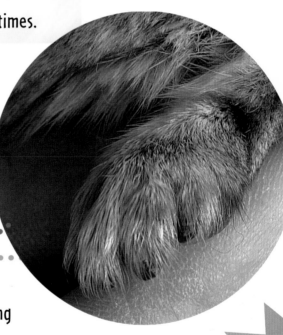

Top tip

You should never wash your chinchilla. Washing a chinchilla will cause more harm than good because it will destroy its fur's natural oils.

Shedding fur

Chinchillas are able to shed their fur if they are grabbed suddenly. This is part of their protection system. Chinchillas living in the wild shed fur to help them escape when they are attacked by other animals, or by birds of prey. They then scurry away to hide under the rocks on the mountain side. The lost fur grows back in about ten to twelve weeks.

Handling your chinchilla

Making friends with your chinchilla takes time. Your pet will need to get to know you, and you will need to become confident about handling it. Remember you are like a giant to your pet! You must do everything slowly and deliberately so you do not frighten or startle it. The more you handle your pet, the more confident it will be that you will not hurt it.

Once your chinchilla feels sure you will not hurt it, it will learn to sit on your lap. Chinchillas love to sit on your lap and be tickled behind the ears. Soon they will begin to explore and very soon they will be climbing up onto your shoulder and nibbling at you!

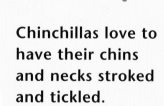

Chinchillas love to have their chins and necks stroked and tickled.

Gaining its trust

- Start by having your chinchilla sit on the upturned palm of your hand when it is in its cage.
- When it is sitting on the upturned palm of your hand, gently lift it towards the cage door.
- At first it may jump off your hand and you will have to start all over again.

When it does let you lift it out of its cage you will know that you have made a friend of your chinchilla.

Tail alert!

Never try to catch your chinchilla by grabbing at its tail. You will probably find that it escapes and you are left with just a small piece of tail fur in your hand!

Out of the cage

When holding your chinchilla, whether it is sitting on your hand or resting on your forearm, if you want to stop it getting away you can gently hold onto its tail (see picture on right).

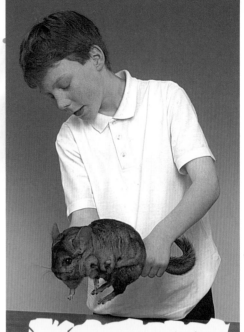

Always hold your chinchilla's tail at the end nearest to its bottom. If you don't you could damage it.

It is important when holding your pet that you don't squeeze it tightly. It won't like this and will try to get away if you are rough with it. It may even nip or bite you.

When holding your chinchilla you must always be gentle and very patient.

Safety first

If your chinchilla nips or scratches you, tell an adult. You should wash the bite or scratch with some cotton wool dipped in mild antiseptic.

Exercise time

Try to set aside some time every day for your pet to play outside its cage. While your chinchilla is running around, make sure you stay with it all the time, so it cannot get into trouble or get lost. Your chinchilla will like to race around the edges of your room, next to the walls, so try to create a clear 'run' for your pet!

Preparing your room

Your chinchilla will love exploring, but before you let it out of its cage, you will need to prepare for its exercise time.

- Make sure there are no open windows that your chinchilla could climb out of.
- Block up any holes or loose floorboards that your pet might be tempted to investigate.
- Make sure there are no buckets of water or toilets that your pet can fall into. Chinchillas cannot swim. Their fur will get waterlogged and the chinchilla will quickly drown.
- Keep electric cables out of reach of your pet. Chinchillas can gnaw through cables very easily so, to be extra careful, turn off any electrical equipment in the room.
- Remove any precious objects or things that would be bad for your chinchilla to chew on.
- If you have cats or dogs, put them in another room. They will frighten your chinchilla.

Make sure your pet cannot nibble any plants. They may be poisonous!

It is a good idea to stay with your pet all the time so it cannot get into trouble or get lost.

Catching your chinchilla

Sometimes your chinchilla will not come to you when you want to put it back in its cage. If this happens, try to block off a small section of the room. Then offer your pet the palm of your hand so that it can step onto it. You may need to tempt your chinchilla with a single raisin to encourage it to step onto your hand.

If your chinchilla still refuses to come to you, place a carrying cage on the floor next to a straight part of the wall. Now guide your pet into it, using a piece of cardboard or plywood to form an avenue to the door of the carrying cage.

If your pet does not want to be picked up, it may help to offer it a small treat. Never grab at your chinchilla. You will only frighten it.

Some health problems

Chinchillas rarely suffer from illnesses and diseases, but sometimes your pet may get ill. Here are a few of the problems that could affect your chinchilla's health.

Upset stomach

If your chinchilla's droppings are small, runny and wet, it has an upset stomach. This may be caused by mouldy hay. Do not feed your pet any more hay for three to four days. Also, make certain that it has plenty of pellets to eat and fresh water to drink. It should recover in a few days, but if it does not, take it to the vet.

This chinchilla is obviously healthy and **alert**. If your chinchilla sits quietly in the corner of its cage and takes no notice of you, it may be ill.

Eye problems

Sometimes, when chinchillas use their dust bath they may get a little sand in one of their eyes. The eye may become sore and even close up. If this happens, bathe the eye gently with warm water. This should help to clear the eye. However, if some pus comes out, the eye has become infected and it should be seen by a vet.

If your chinchilla's eye becomes infected, you should take it to a vet as soon as possible.

Cuts

Chinchillas rarely cut themselves, but if your pet does get a small cut, you should bathe the injury gently with a piece of cotton wool dipped in warm water. Do not try to cover the wound with a plaster or dressing, because your pet will only chew it off. If your pet has a serious cut, you should take it to the vet immediately.

Heat stroke

If the temperature rises to 20°C, it will start to get too hot for your pet. If your chinchilla is suffering from too much heat, it will probably be lying down and breathing heavily and its ears will be very pink. You must act quickly. If possible, take your pet to a cooler room. Make sure there is plenty of cool air circulating in the room. A fan can help to cool down your pet. Give it plenty of water to drink. If it does not recover, contact the vet.

Chinchillas cannot take their fur coats off, so when the temperature rises they can get dangerously hot.

Fur fungus

Fur fungus is highly **contagious**. This means it can be passed on easily from one chinchilla to another. If you suspect that your chinchilla has fur fungus, you should **isolate** it immediately, keeping it away from other chinchillas.

A chinchilla with fur fungus will have bald patches on its body. The bald patches will have pimples and blisters on them and will look very sore. Usually the fungus starts around the nose, chin, eyes and ears. It is not a **fatal** disease – your pet will not die from it, but it will make your chinchilla unhappy. Pets with fur fungus lose weight and can become bad tempered.

Top tip

- If you suspect that your chinchilla has fur fungus, you should take it to the vet, who will give you advice on how to treat it.
- As well as treating your pet with ointment or medicine, you should also wash out its cage and all its equipment with hot soapy water and a mild disinfectant.

If you are worried about your chinchilla's health you should take it to the vet. You will need to transport your chinchilla in a suitable carry cage. Make sure that it cannot chew its way out.

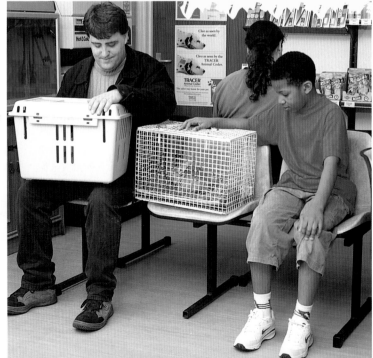

Fur chewing

You may notice that your chinchilla has started to chew its fur. No one knows for sure what causes fur chewing in chinchillas. Some people believe that chinchillas start biting their fur because they are nervous, because they do not have a well-balanced diet, or because they are not happy in the place that they are kept.

If your chinchilla starts biting its fur, try to think if something might be upsetting it. Perhaps you have changed its pellets or not given it hay every day? You may have changed the position of its cage so it no longer feels secure. Or maybe it just wants more attention from you?

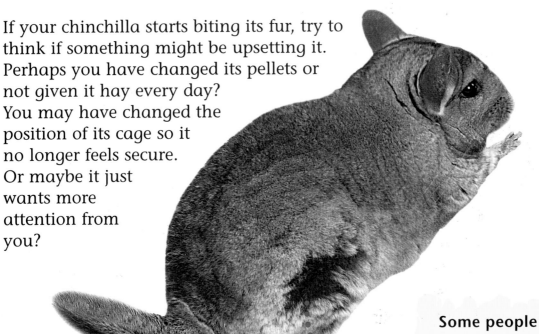

Some people think that chinchillas chew their fur because they do not like to be too quiet! They believe that the sound of a radio helps to keep chinchillas calm.

Catching chinchilla diseases

Can humans catch chinchilla diseases from chinchillas? The answer is no – chinchillas have not been known to pass on any diseases to humans. However, you should always wash your hands after handling your chinchilla or cleaning its cage. You could get an upset stomach from touching its waste and droppings.

Visiting the vet

Sometimes you will need to take your chinchilla to the vet. You should know your vet's address and telephone number in case of an emergency. These are some of the problems that your vet might need to deal with.

Teeth problems

Like all **rodents**, chinchillas have teeth that keep on growing throughout their life. Rodents need to gnaw on things all the time, to stop their teeth from growing too long. However, even if you provide lots of chewing blocks for your chinchilla, it can still develop teeth problems.

The vet will need to give your pet a thorough physical examination.

Warning signs

These are some of the signs that your pet may have tooth trouble.

- Your chinchilla's **incisors** (front teeth) may be **overgrown** or may not be growing straight.
- Your pet may have runny eyes. It may be dribbling from its mouth, and down its neck and chest.
- It may be losing weight.
- It may be pawing at its mouth.

Malocclusion

If your pet is in obvious pain from toothache, it may be suffering from **malocclusion**. This is a problem that happens when a chinchilla's teeth do not grow properly, and, sadly, there is no cure for it. Animals with malocclusion can suffer badly. Their teeth can grow into their head or into the back of their eyes and jaws as well as into their mouth. They will have great difficulty eating their pellets and hay.

If your pet develops malocclusion, you will need to see your vet and maybe have your pet put to sleep. Although this will be sad for you, it is much better for your pet than letting it suffer. Happily most chinchillas do not develop this problem.

Ear problems

If your chinchilla is constantly scratching its ears, this could be a sign of a problem developing. You should take your chinchilla to a vet. If your chinchilla has any obvious problems with its ears, such as a smelly **discharge** (liquid coming out of its ears) or wetness, you should contact your vet immediately. The vet may give you ear drops to put in your pet's ears or may suggest that you give it some **antibiotics** to clear up the problem.

This vet has a special instrument that lets her see into the animal's ears.

Saying goodbye

Chinchillas can live for up to twenty years, but one day, no matter how well you care for your pet, it will die. Sometimes a chinchilla will die peacefully and unexpectedly at home. This will come as a shock to you, but do not blame yourself. There is probably nothing that you could have done.

When chinchillas get old, they become less energetic and spend more time sleeping. This chinchilla is old, but it is still in good condition.

A peaceful end

As a caring owner, the hardest responsibility of all is to know when to let your pet be put to sleep to save it from suffering. Your chinchilla may be very old and in pain. Or it may have a serious illness which cannot be cured. Your vet will give it a small injection. This does not hurt, it just makes your pet sleepy. Before you can count to ten, your chinchilla will be asleep and then its heart will stop beating. If you can, your pet will appreciate you cuddling it as it falls asleep.

Feeling upset

However it happens, you will feel upset when a pet dies, especially if your chinchilla has been a friend for many years. It is perfectly normal for people, adults as well as children, to cry when a pet dies, or when they think of a dead pet.

Sometimes it helps to have a special burial place for your pet. Eventually, the pain will pass and you will be left with happy memories of your chinchilla.

Looking after your chinchilla will have taught you a lot about these lovable animals. Maybe you will be able to give a home to another chinchilla that needs love and care?

Keeping a record

It is fun to keep a record of your chinchilla. Buy a big scrapbook and fill it with notes and photos. Then you can look back at all the things you and your pet did together. Your chinchilla scrapbook can include information that you might need when you take your pet to the vet, or if you enter your pet for chinchilla shows.

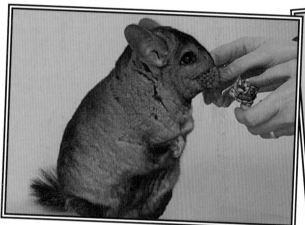

You can take photos of your pet doing all sorts of things, and then choose the best ones to put in your scrapbook.

A special diary

You could start your scrapbook with the first day that you saw your pet, who you bought it from and how old it was. You can note down special events in the life of your pet, such as the first time you saw it take a dust bath, the first day it sat on your lap or on your shoulders and the first time you tried to groom it. You can make a note of the funny things your chinchilla does. If you enter your chinchilla for shows, you could make notes on the shows you go to – and the prizes it wins!

Chinchillas shows

Some people take their chinchillas to shows.

- Shows are held throughout Great Britain, the USA, Canada, Australia and Europe.
- Judges decide which chinchillas are in the best condition and have the best shape and fur.
- There are societies that specialize in show-quality chinchillas. You can find addresses for these societies on page 47.

If you look after your chinchilla properly, you will both have a lot of fun together!

Useful information

If you bought your chinchilla from a **breeder**, you may have a **pedigree** document, with details of who its mother and father were. Your breeder may also tell you about members of your pet's family that won ribbons or awards. This is all good information to put in your scrapbook.

You might decide to collect magazine articles about chinchillas. Cut them out and keep them in your scrapbook. They will soon build up into a good store of tips and guidance.

Glossary

allergy   sensitive reaction to something, which can make your skin itch or make you sneeze

alert   lively and interested in everything

antibiotics   medicine that fights infection

breed   to keep animals and encourage them to mate so they produce young

breeder   someone who keeps animals and encourages them to mate and produce young

contagious   passed on by touching or coming into close contact with something

crevice   gap or crack in a rock

cylindrical   shaped like a tube or a cylinder

deformed   crooked, or bent out of shape

discharge   liquid coming out of somewhere, such as an animal's ear

domesticate   to tame an animal, so that it can live with people

endangered   in danger of dying out

fatal   deadly

galvanized   treated to prevent rust

groom   to clean an animal's coat by brushing or combing it; animals often groom themselves

illegal   against the law

incisors   front teeth

isolate   keep apart from other animals or humans

kit   young chinchilla

mammal   animal with fur or hair on its body that feeds its babies with milk

malocclusion   disease that prevents teeth from growing straight

moult   to lose fur at particular times of year, usually spring or summer

nocturnal   active at night

overgrown   grown too long

pedigree   document giving the names of an animal's parents

prime   the time of life when an animal is at its strongest and in its best condition

protected species   group of animals that is protected from hunters by law

retaining clip   clip that holds something firmly in place

rodent   animal with strong front teeth for gnawing

roughage   food that takes a long time to digest and helps people and animals to stay healthy

suckle   to drink milk from a mother

urine   liquid (pee) passed out of the body containing water and waste substances

vitamins   important substances found in food that help people and animals to stay healthy

volcanic   from an area with volcanoes

warm-blooded   an animal that is able to create its own body heat

weaned   ready to eat solid food and stop drinking the mother's milk

Useful addresses

Most countries have national chinchilla societies, which give helpful advice on caring for your pet. As well as these large organizations there are also smaller chinchilla clubs. Look for their address in your telephone book, or in your local library. You could also ask your vet or your pet shop owner about a local chinchilla club.

National Chinchilla Society (NCS)

The NCS has a website:
www.national-chinchilla-soc.freeserve.co.uk
The society publishes a paper called the *Gazette* and leaflets on topics related to chinchillas. It organizes field days at which knowledgeable members of the society give talks and displays. It also organizes shows for all members and their pets.

More books to read

This is a list of books about chinchillas for adults. Most of them are simple guides that an adult can help you read.

Getting to Know Your Chinchilla, Gill Page (Interpet Publishing, 2001)
Guide to Owning a Chinchilla, Anmarie Barrie (TFH Publications, 1997)
Pet Owners Guide to the Chinchilla, Natalie Kirkiewicz and Gary Broomhead (Ringpress Books, 1998)
Your First Chinchilla, Roger Whear (Kingdom Books, 1999)

Helpful websites

www.chinnet.net – contains lots of advice about how to look after your pet, including information about where you can find a good chinchilla dealer in your area.

Index